My Muslim Community

Kate Taylor and Faiza Qureshi

Photography by Chris Fairclough

FRANKLIN WATTS
LONDON • SYDNEY

First published in 2005 by
Franklin Watts
96 Leonard Street
London
EC2A 4XD

Franklin Watts Australia
45-51 Huntley Street
Alexandria
NSW 2015

ISBN: 0 7496 5881 9

A CIP catalogue record for this book
is available from the British Library

Printed in Malaysia
Planning and production by Discovery Books Limited
Editor: Laura Durman
Designer: Ian Winton

The author, packager and publisher would like to thank the following people for their
participation in this book:
   The Qureshi family
   Zeenat and Samia Latif
   Samia and Madiha Ashraf
   Ajaz Ahmed
   Bobbersmill Community Centre
   Sayab Kayani
   Shahzad Ghani
   Medina Store
   Mughal Store
   Kasmir Halal Meat
   Umani
   Nottingham Islamia School
   Dr M Hussain (Director Karimia Institute)
   Samina Qayyum
   The Islamic Centre
   Majid Ash-Shifa mosque

Contents

All About Me

My name is Faiza Qureshi and I am 9 years old. I am a *Muslim* and I live in Forest Fields, in Nottingham.

Lots of Muslims live here. Most of the younger ones were born here like me.

I live with my parents, my two sisters and my two brothers. My mum, Shama, and my dad, Iqbal, share their room with my 3-year-old brother, Haroon. Mohsin, my elder brother, is 24 and has his own room in the attic.

▲ **My family outside our house.**

I share a room with my sisters, Madihah, who is 13, and Samihah, who is 12.

◄ **This is our bedroom.**

My Family

Most of my family live in Pakistan, and I have been to see them twice.

My parents are from Mirpur in Pakistan. They moved to Nottingham 25 years ago. Dad is a builder and has his own company. Mum works at home, cooking, cleaning and looking after the family.

On special occasions, like when Haroon was born, my relatives come over from Pakistan to visit us.

▶ **My parents.**

My cousin Hajra lives just around the corner. She's 9 like me. We play at each other's houses all the time.

▶ **My cousin Hajra.**

◀ **My older brother Mohsin.**

Where I Live

Forest Fields is a really lively place to live. There are some nice shops and I can walk to school easily.

There's a school at the end of my road called Forest Fields Primary School. It's not the school I go to every day, but on Saturdays I learn *Urdu* there.

▶ **I live in this road.**

Bobbersmill has a great Muslim community centre. It's about five minutes away from my house by car. There's a *mosque* where we go to pray, and a sports hall where I have PE lessons with the school. It's also got a Muslim radio station called Radio Faza that we listen to at home.

▲ **The community centre at Bobbersmill.**

◄ **A DJ at Radio Faza.**

Markets and Shops

I like going shopping, and there are lots of different shops in Nottingham.

We get most of our food from Asda but we also go to local shops. My favourite is called Medina, where we buy Pakistani food, spices and vegetables.

▶▼ **Medina is really big inside!**

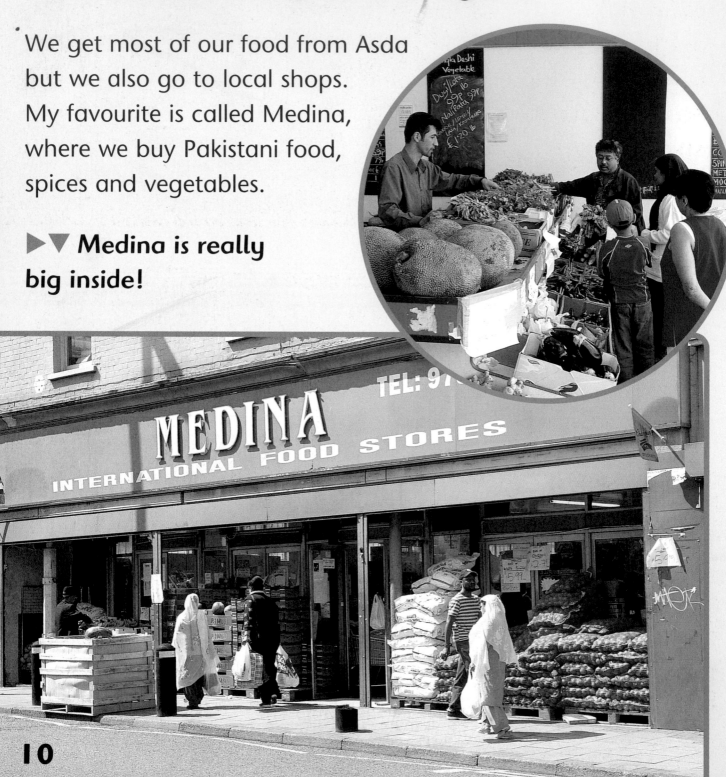

Muslims have to get meat from special butchers, called *halal* butchers. We go to a shop called Kashmir Halal Meat in Hyson Green.

In the local fabric shops, you can have outfits made. Someone measures you and you tell them which material you want. Lots of people shop there, not just Muslims.

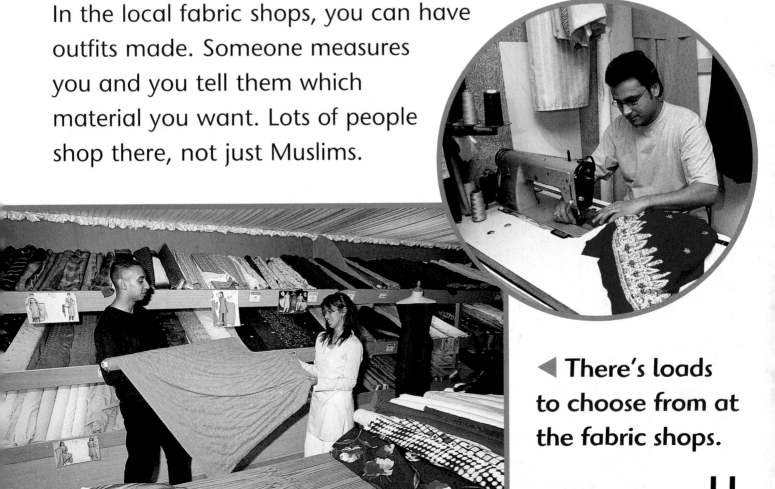

◀ **There's loads to choose from at the fabric shops.**

11

My School

My school is called the Nottingham Islamia School. Lots of Muslims go there.

We learn the same things as other children but also learn about our religion. My favourite subjects are science and maths. I think geography is quite boring.

▼ My teacher.

At break I like to play games, and my favourite is called polo. Someone stands on one side of the playground and, when they shout, we all have to run to the other side as fast as we can without being caught.

My legs ache afterwards, but I'm one of the fastest runners in the class so I don't usually get caught.

▲ **My friends playing polo.**

My Friends

Because I go to a Muslim school, most of my friends are Muslims like me.

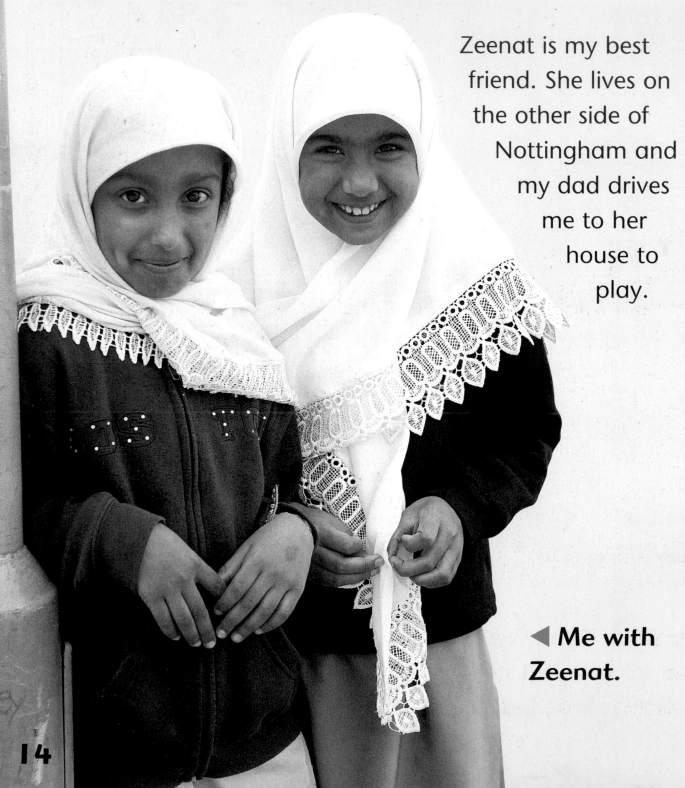

Zeenat is my best friend. She lives on the other side of Nottingham and my dad drives me to her house to play.

◄ Me with Zeenat.

14

My friends Samia and Madiha live across the road. They are twins. We play together after school and at weekends.

▼ **Samia (far left) and Madiha (standing).**

When I'm in year 6, I'll go to the English school my older sisters go to and will probably make lots of non-Muslim friends.

Food

My favourite meal is roast chicken with mashed potatoes – I wish I could have that every day.

My mum makes really nice Pakistani food like *curry*, rice and *chapattis*. I eat a lot of meat, but never any pork. Muslims aren't allowed to eat meat from pigs.

▼ **We like to eat our meals together.**

I love crisp sandwiches. Sometimes I take plain bread and butter to school so I can make them for lunch. They're delicious!

I try to learn how to cook from my mum. I enjoy it.

My Hobbies

I have lots of hobbies, and I love playing with my friends when I'm not at school.

I really like art and sometimes try to make things at home.

I use different materials, like paint and pipe cleaners. I have lots of different coloured glitter too!

◀ My picture of a mosque.

I play games like cat's cradle with my friends, and I enjoy playing out in the garden in the summer.

My favourite TV programme is 'Tracy Beaker'. I watch the Cartoon Network a lot with my little brother Haroon because he really likes it.

◀ **Me and Haroon watching TV.**

19

Languages

I can speak two different languages: English and a Pakistani language called Urdu.

I speak English most of the time, but on Saturday I have Urdu lessons with a Pakistani teacher. I get cross when I can't think of the right words. My parents would like me to study Urdu at university, but I want to be a *pharmacist*.

▶ **At the community centre, I try to read the posters written in Urdu.**

My dad understands English but doesn't speak it very well. Mum doesn't understand it at all so I talk to her in Urdu.

Haroon has started learning English at nursery and can write his name now.

▲ **Chatting to Mum in Urdu.**

◀ **Doing my Urdu homework.**

Clothes

I wear an outfit called a _salwar kameez_ most of the time. My favourite one is red and gold.

Muslim girls and women aren't allowed to wear tight-fitting clothing, so the salwar kameez has a loose top. When I go to activities at Forest Fields Primary School in the holidays, with children who aren't Muslim, I wear jeans and jumpers.

I have lots of different coloured bracelets to wear with my outfits.

Muslim boys sometimes wear a salwar kameez too, but usually in colours like beige, grey and white.

My dad always wears Western clothes, but my mum usually wears a salwar kameez.

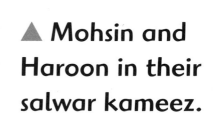

▲ Mohsin and Haroon in their salwar kameez.

◄ Me and my friends usually wear a headscarf with our salwar kameez.

Religion

My religion is called Islam and the people who follow it are called Muslims.

We believe that God sent prophets to show us how to live. The last prophet was Muhammed (*peace be upon him*). His message is written in our holy book, the Qur'an.

▶ **Me reading the Qur'an.**

I pray in the mosque at Bobbersmill, but there are quite a lot of other mosques in Nottingham. I always cover my head with a scarf as a sign of respect to God.

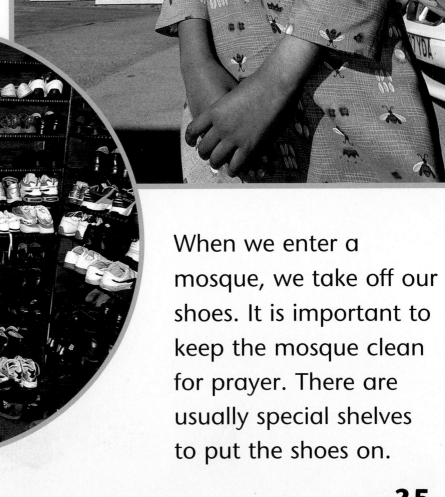

When we enter a mosque, we take off our shoes. It is important to keep the mosque clean for prayer. There are usually special shelves to put the shoes on.

Prayer

Prayer is important to Muslims, and we pray at special times throughout the day.

Adult Muslims have to pray five times every day. When we pray we kneel on the floor or on a mat and face the direction of the holy city of *Mecca*.

◀ Me and my family praying in the mosque at Bobbersmill.

The first prayer is at 5 in the morning. I pray at school during lunchtime and then with my family when I get home. My parents pray twice more, late at night, when I've gone to bed.

Radio Faza plays a special prayer, called the adhan, when it is time to pray so we don't forget.

◀ **This is the *muezzin* at our mosque. He calls Muslims to prayer by chanting the adhan.**

Celebrations

Muslims celebrate two main festivals called Eid ul-Fitr and Eid ul-Adha.

Ramadan is the ninth month of the Muslim calendar. During Ramadan, we go to the mosque a lot to pray. We also fast, which means we don't eat or drink from sunrise to sunset. In the evening we have a feast.

We believe that fasting cleanses the body. Children, though, are allowed to eat fruit during the day.

When Ramadan is over we have the festival of Eid ul-Fitr. We say special prayers and cook lovely food. We also get new clothes to wear to the mosque.

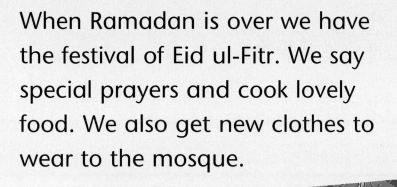

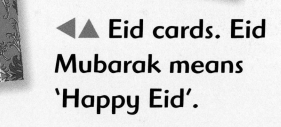

◀◀▲ Eid cards. Eid Mubarak means 'Happy Eid'.

Eid ul-Adha means 'Festival of Sacrifice'. We remember the story about the prophet *Ibrahim* (peace be upon him) who was willing to sacrifice his son when God asked him to. A lot of Muslims go to Mecca during Eid ul-Adha.

I like Nottingham

Living in Nottingham is really good. I have lots of friends and go to a nice school. My parents like it too because lots of people from their town in Pakistan live here. I wouldn't like to live anywhere else.

Glossary

Chapatti A thin Indian bread.

Curry An Indian or Pakistani dish of meat or vegetables flavoured with spices and usually eaten with rice.

Halal The meat from animals that have been killed in a special way for Muslims.

Ibrahim A prophet, also known as Abraham in the Old Testament. God ordered him to sacrifice his son Isma'il (or Isaac) to test his faith. Ibrahim was willing to do so, but just before he made the sacrifice, God told him to kill a ram instead.

Mecca A city in Saudi Arabia. It is the holiest place in the world for a Muslim. Every Muslim tries to go there once in their lifetime.

Mosque The building in which Muslims worship.

Muezzin The Muslim official who calls people to prayer.

Muslim A person who follows the religion called Islam.

Peace be upon him Whenever Muslims mention the name of a prophet, they say this phrase as a sign of respect.

Pharmacist A person who prepares and dispenses medicines.

Salwar kameez A loose tunic top and trousers.

Urdu The official language of Pakistan, also spoken in parts of India.

Index